Rough Fugue

SOUTHERN MESSENGER POETS
Dave Smith, Series Editor

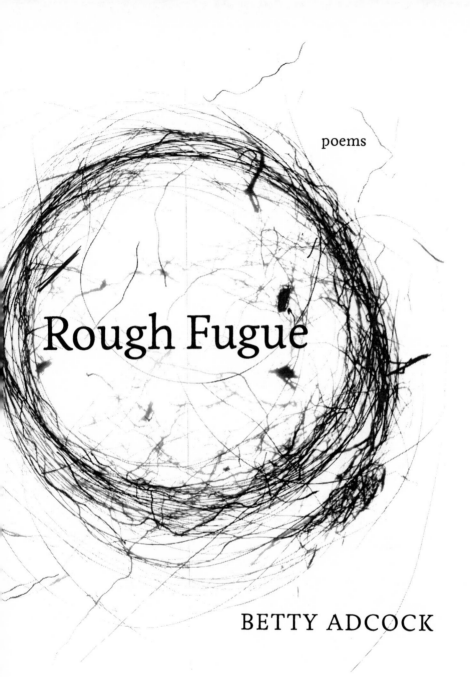

poems

Rough Fugue

BETTY ADCOCK

LOUISIANA STATE UNIVERSITY PRESS   BATON ROUGE

1-27-19

Published by Louisiana State University Press
Copyright © 2017 by Betty Adcock
All rights reserved
Manufactured in the United States of America
LSU Press Paperback Original
FIRST PRINTING

Designer: Barbara Neely Bourgoyne
Typeface: Adobe Minion Pro, text; Livory, display
Printer and binder: LSI

LIBRARY OF CONGRESS CATALOGING-IN-PUBLICATION DATA
Names: Adcock, Betty, author.
Title: Rough fugue : poems / Betty Adcock.
Description: Baton Rouge : Louisiana State University Press, [2017] | Series:
  Southern Messenger Poets
Identifiers: LCCN 2017005126| ISBN 978-0-8071-6668-0 (pbk. : alk. paper) |
  ISBN 978-0-8071-6669-7 (pdf) | ISBN 978-0-8071-6670-3 (epub)
Classification: LCC PS3551.D396 A6 2017 | DDC 811/.54—dc23
LC record available at https://lccn.loc.gov/2017005126

This book is for my husband

DONALD ADCOCK
June 24, 1925–May 10, 2011

and for

CLAUDIA EMERSON
January 13, 1957–December 4, 2014

CONTENTS

Acknowledgments   ix

ARGUMENTS

Talisman   3

No Encore   4

Meditation/Elegy   5

River   7

Word for the 21st Century   8

Small Prayer   9

Photography 1   10

Photography 2   12

Joe Mike   14

Transport   16

Hold   17

Evidence   18

WIDOW POEMS

Circle   21

Lunar: A History   23

Vulpine   25

The Widow's House   27

The Widow Tries to
Say It without Philosophy,
Theology, or Grief   28

The Widow Remembers That
Someone Once Said   30

The Widow Reverses
Wordsworth   31

The Widow Finds the
Annuals   33

Clearing   34

Reach   36

GARMENT OF LIGHT

If Their Voices   39

Rising Star 1984   40

Burnt Offerings   42

Pastoral   43

After Despair   45

Colloquy   46

Song for Mary Ellen   47

Ode to a Shawl   48

Office Cubicle   49

The Drifter Picked Up at
the Dump   50

Ode to a Guinea Pig   51

Parking Lot   53

Photography 3   54

Survivals   55

Articles of Faith   58

Notes   61

ACKNOWLEDGMENTS

Poems in this book originally appeared, sometimes in slightly different forms or with different titles, in the following publications:

Birmingham Review: "Pastoral," "Evidence," "Found," and "Small Prayer"; *Blackbird*: "Transport" and "Word for the 21st Century"; *Cortland Review*: "The Widow Tries to Say It without Philosophy, Theology, or Grief," "Joe Mike," "River," "Ode to a Guinea Pig," and "No Encore"; *Great River Review*: "Burnt Offerings" and "Vulpine"; *Inch*: "After Despair"; *NEO*: "Circle" and "Parking Lot"; *New South*: "If Their Voices"; *Pleiades*: "Rising Star."

"Colloquy" appeared in the Anthology *The Rag-Picker's Guide to Poetry*, University of Michigan Press, 2013.

"Lunar: A History" appeared in the anthology *... and Love...*, Jacar Press, 2013.

"Vulpine" appeared in the anthology *Intimacy*, Jacar Press, 2015.

"Rising Star," "Burnt Offerings," and "If Their Voices" appeared in the anthology *Hard Lines; Rough South*, University of South Carolina Press, 2016.

"Small Prayer" appeared in the anthology *What Matters*, Jacar Press, 2014.

The section titled "Widow Poems" appeared as a chapbook from Jacar Press in 2014.

I owe thanks to Nora Shepard, Noel Crook, Kelly Michaels, Elizabeth Jackson, Shannon Ward, Al Maginnes, Deborah Pope, and especially my daughter Sylvia. I owe particular thanks to Timothy McBride, whose kindness helped me back to writing.

Arguments

Poetry is a species of thought with which nothing else can be done.

—HOWARD NEMEROV

Talisman

Half-buried in gravel and winter
on a dawn-damp Colorado trail,
the elk antler trembled as I dug it out, then
woke in my hand like a dowser's wand—

and has kept now twenty years
a ceaseless peace on my bookshelf,
being in this room the one power
that is wordless.

It traces a memory of rivers,
branching as if the path it has traveled,
dead end after dead end,
is the only way into the high places.

Chill to the touch, smelling of an other
earth both vanished and wholly present,
yellowish, streaked white, ribbed
with shadow like old snow, it's the rough
image of the night-tined candelabra
whose blown fire led me to see in the dark.

No Encore

I'm just an assistant with the Vanishing Act.
My spangled wand points out the disappeared.
It's only a poor thing made of words, and lacks
the illusive power to light the darkling year.

Not prophecy, not elegy, but fact:
the thing that's gone is never coming back.

Late or soon a guttering silence will ring down
a curtain like woven smoke on thickening air.
The audience will strain to see what's there,
the old magician nowhere to be found.

For now, I wear a costume and dance obliquely.
The applause you hear is not for me, its rabid sound
like angry rain—as one by one the known forms cease to be:
childhood, the farm, the river, forested ground;
the tiger and the condor, the whale, the honeybee;
the village, the book, the lantern. Then you. Then me.

Meditation/Elegy

The greatest poverty is not to live
in a physical world, to feel one's desire
is too difficult to tell from despair.
    —Wallace Stevens

All words contain a tree,
language a rooted branching
on the paths of breath.
The word for *book* began with Latin
liber, name for the inner bark
of certain trees the early Romans found
to be the best material for writing on.

Like all things, its first body was of earth,
plain clay furrowed with cuneiform,
Ur-epic baked onto tablets made stronger
by the fires of time and war. *Gilgamesh,*
dug from millennia at Nineveh, that story still
incised anew with every generation.

The waters, too, had part in this: scrolls
of papyrus five hundred thousand strong
at Alexandria, where Strato and Euclid
and Eratosthenes, scientists and philosophers,
poets and dreamers gathered where the books
were gathered, where the Nile's reeds made
cradles for history and change.

Vellum came, and parchment, the membrane
between ourselves and other creatures thinner
than we knew, and then alight with golden flowers,
bright animals and birds, saints, seasons and blue heaven's

promise—art and language in a dance, world
reflected, made, remade, undone,
returning—tethered still to origin.

What breathless Babel rises now with our desire,
in our despair? What immaterial tower?

River

Here some people put a bridge.
Then somebody broke it.
Somebody put it back.
It happens and happens.

Now people look and photograph.
Below, children are playing on a raft—
it's still a river,
but nobody crosses at this place anymore.

This could be a story about love.
Or poetry. Or war.

Word for the 21st Century

Her teacher spelled the word *water* into the hand
of the blind and deaf child while water coursed
over their palms. It was the first word.

In the unbreakable summers,
heat muffles even the stars
in their stalled dark. No smallest
wind touches days that are empty
as the ears of the deaf, days colored
that pale red closed eyes can see.
Our hands are open but blank,
their rivering prophecies erased.

Heat pulls the lakes and streams
out of their beds and takes them elsewhere.
Songbirds fall straight from dulled air
into the dying flowers.
                              This time,
the blind and unhearing will learn
water not by touch but by absence,
in a silence whose name is thirst.

Small Prayer

We see this ground as if through a spaceship's
faceted metal eye. Having seen the blue round
as small as a child's ball, having solved just enough
of mystery to be lost in what we think
we know. We've thought to play with it,
to make the planet smaller yet.

Now we do with it what we will,
forgetting how its vastness left us
speechless, worshipping. We lose
forest and furrow where we began.
And the kindred animals have begun
to leave. The water's gone
that married time and loved the stone
into a canyon's grace. We've forgotten
how to stay—how to say: *this place.*

Let the earth grow large enough again
that only clouds and stories can
encircle it entire. Let rockets land
for good, satellites fall dumb,
and wires unspan enough that distances
grow wide to dwarf our wars.
May mystery loom large enough again
to answer prayers and keep us.

Photography 1
1879

They are here, handwritten in old light.
How precisely in that sun's brown script
they bend at the waist in lace and pale cream,
in ruffles and wide hats with wind-lifted ribbons
like small flags stalled in their drift.

The tall cane fence ran alongside then,
and the summerhouse slumbered in a corner
of this square window into a century
vanished so long that another has opened
and closed its slow shutter. A spring

or summer day (trees leafed and serving
the moment) has caught them out in this ghost
of my great-grandfather's deer park,
a gentleman farmer's folly, his ladies
haunting the half-grown fawns

who put up their heads to be stroked,
pets—as the women are—kept
close and thought pretty in the confining.
Everything's here, even one cloud
like a smudge of smoke, even

a small snarl of real smoke that must have come
from the cabin at the edge of that field,
out of the picture, a captivity not suitable
for inclusion in this precious
staying of unreliable light.

The women will not look up or warn us.
The moment has them utterly, rests lightly
on the absurd hats, the sepia grass, the unbroken
sky benign except for its unfinished sentence.

Photography 2

Sylvia Hudgins Sharp, 1900–1944

Photographs of her have overshadowed memory.
I do remember terror the last time I saw my mother,
as if terror were a light that fixed an image hard;
that clear, that permanent.
The album's snapshots, taking the place
of sound, color, the motion of possibility,
remind my childhood—small squares with white borders.

In the one image that's not a photograph, my mother
is in her coffin, her beautiful black hair with its early
wing of white spread against pink satin, vivid colors
in the parlor wallpaper, bright fragrance of roses,
the dim lamps, the night black at the windows.

I had waked crying for her, and someone
had carried me in my pajamas, lifted to see
the stillness she'd become.
                                        The creaking
of our old house would have been the same
as it was that afternoon or morning, but now
people sat all around in chairs with flowers
everywhere, flowers and people strangely mixed,
voices I didn't know blending like smoke.
I was six years old.

Photographs have a way of displacing whatever else
there might have been. I've lost the sound of her voice,
though it must have meant all speech to me—
every day she read to me from a set of books I've kept:
Literature for Children in seven volumes.

In the keepsake snapshots, she wears a white sunhat in the garden,
holds my puppy at the gate, lights a birthday candle, stands
by a Christmas tree. In one picture we're sitting in the porch swing.
I'm looking up at her as she reads from the open book
in her lap, her mouth opening on a word.
Even now, I can thumb through that volume yellow with age
and find a presence, almost a scent. Perhaps the salt of her hands
stayed among the stories and inked illustrations.

The photograph that's not a photograph
is the one that stays, burned into my life
one October night in 1944.
It displaces nothing, being itself a ghost,
the only image that could not stop time;
acknowledges no past, kindling still
the moving picture I go on holding fast.

Joe Mike

Boys were given double names in deep East Texas,
where everything needed repeated force
just to stand out, to be dragged out of the dense
forests and rutted country roads.
And these weren't nicknames but were inscribed
in the baptismal rolls of clapboard churches—
Jimmy Clyde, Bill Tom, Herbert Gene.
Like all of them, you grew into the heaviest jobs,
the most to lose.

Working the night shift repairing power lines
one icy December, you grabbed with both hands
the live lightning. What must it have been like
to grasp, like Prometheus, the fire—
without the power to give it away?
Was there a sudden shimmer of knowledge,
something understood? or only the instant's slippage
swift as a wind-struck candle into night,
before you could know that surge?

The surgeons took both your hands.

You'd been the boy who always smiled,
bulky, clumsy, no good at sports, and teased
as such boys always are, but laughing
to make up for what you weren't.
When I saw you for the first time in fifty years,
you hid the hooks, refused to eat
in front of us. And when I reached
to embrace you—*No!* you said and would not
let me touch you.

Later I learned about your only son,
a champion buckle-winning bull rider,
who blew his brains out at twenty-four in Colorado.

You, who had held onto so much power
it should have killed you, had carried that current
like the remnant of a god and it had broken off
as if a luminous spear had snapped inside you,
leaving a pitch-black permanence,
the light and dark unparted, doubled and doubled again
until *there was no light. There was no light at all.*

Transport

Driving any country road at night, you'll come
upon one—rabbit, possum, skunk, raccoon—
run over again and again, become a stretched shadow
flat as a footprint saying its only direction.

Because I've left behind so many,
because I have memories of my own
small claws and brittle bone, this time
I paid attention to the breath
of impulse at my neck and stopped
just this once, backed up the car and walked
in braked light to a tangle of animal

recently struck and just recognizable.
It draped like cloth in my hands, boneless,
wet with its life in a smell not yet of decay
but of shorted-out heat, electric.
I laid bloody splinters and fur in roadside brush,
then wiped my hands on ditch-weeds in the dark
where I couldn't name anything.

Now the road held just a thick stain
to burn out in tomorrow's noon.
I thought of my own veins branching,
the working of intricate connections,
the laying down of ways of return—

and I drove on, my travels
raveling behind in a thickening
darkness broken by nothing
for miles but the risen
one-way moon.

Hold

We have to be torn, self by self, away—
the world clasps us that hard—until at last,
no longer able to keep its grip, it must
let go despite briars and sunsets, long
fingers of hurt and light that grasp and grasp;
despite stars and rainstorms and sweet moss,
the orb-web days that catch us up dawn-lit,
dew-strewn, struggling and star-crossed.

Tenacious, tentacled, altogether determined
material spirit: bare hands of the oak tree,
fist of the thunder, little feet of the lizard, all
vying, vying—though none of these can hold,
not summer's golden sway, nor winter's play
on this: *us, dying.*

Evidence

Imagine a box. Imagine it made
of ordinary and exotic woods—say
yellow pine and rosewood, hickory,
chestnut, ebony, teak, a haphazard,
shape-shifting casket expanding to hold

my life and yours, whole landscapes
of stone and river, or sand and wind.
It can contract to the size of a seashell,
to the size of the sound cupped
in a goat bell hung in an olive tree.

This box may hold that Montana mountain
and the star-drilled sky above Siphnos,
the rain-pale air over Derry, an ocean,
an Acropolis, or a white heron in the sun.

I want fishing in the Big Thicket. I want
my father speaking, you laughing, the wild
boar running out of the woods. All of it fits
in the box, both world that was and the one

this moment imagines—the spaceless everything
I've loved, even the wrong ones, all
the befores in place, I've dreamt that story,
the gift.
        Oh, open the box and let be again . . .
even the black wings, carrion, a carillon of crows?

No. Let down the lid and lock it.
Lock it.

Widow Poems

Grief is itself a medicine.

—WILLIAM COWPER

Circle
Don, 2009

That last year, you began to call to each other, as if you were boys
again hallooing across years that lay like fields between you; as if you
blew on grass blades pretending the real instruments that would take
you all the way to music. In high school, you haunted the Durham
Record Store, drunk on the latest
> jazz   blues   big band   cool   beginnings

you beginners trying everything when swing was crazy new.

⁓

1943, the guys in the Navy jazz band you were lucky enough to get
into at seventeen, all shipped out six months later to battles where the
guns' percussion accompanied no tune you'd ever heard, and the only
solos played were kamikazi, I see you in the belly of the battleship
Indiana, waiting, waiting, bored and scared in Damage Control the
third deck down, the bottom from which, if the worst happened, you
never could emerge. There with the hydraulic valves you'd have to turn
to balance the ship if torpedoes hit. You were essential and alone and
you knew it, practicing your flute in the belly of Leviathan—then after
sunrise talking jazz topside over coffee and Spam. Death's possibilities
were always worst at twilight and just before dawn, the battleship's
zigzagging avoidance a wandering as crafty and desperate as Bird's
chords on a hard night.

You made it home, you and Snyder, Kaplan, Zombie, Jay, even Joe
Montagnino, who survived two sunk ships to join you. Now you talked
again. They called from New York, Florida, Atlantic City, Europe—
some of them still playing gigs. They told their ailments, bobbing on
quieter waters beyond the need for rescue, buoyant on rafts of memory
they spoke disappearing into the farthest horizon's setting that is as
brilliant as those they saw from battle stations.

⁓

21

After the Pacific: your life—the education bought with the years
on that fire-riddled ocean. At the university, you boarded at the Skinner
Mansion, an eccentric widow's enormous house. For not much rent,
she put up eight grown men burned by war and passionate for music,
for being alive: Ed, Bernie, Bill, Nut, Bob, Leon, Mims, and you. Sixty
years later you talked to them again, often after decades of nothing said.
They called with cancer, dementia, deaths of spouses. You answered
with surgeries, grandchildren, me. But mostly they said, and you said
back, the names of wonders loved: Parker, Gillespie, Bill Evans, Miles,
Zoot Sims, Sarah Vaughn, Sonny Stitt, riff after riff of praise and rapt
description of some track, some tune: *that solo, that composition, the
incredible chord change, interval, phrasing, control.*

As if you called across the fields of a gone century, boys newly wild to
make again the magic all of you were born for, here where your twilight
was beautiful and dangerous, gathering the blues.

Lunar: A History

In Palomas the moon was Mexican silver, awash
in the dirt street where we danced to mariachi
that rang and shimmered like hammered tin.

Months later on a Dallas sidewalk, an August moon
burned 93 degrees at midnight—imagine—you had come
all that way for this fire.

Outside Abilene we said the September moon
was neon, an Orange Crush sign stopped midflash,
that much-too-sweet, that awful bright.

The next June our East Texas wedding sky
bore an opal cresset sure to carry us
out of one darkness into whatever else there was.

We went straight to Manhattan's summer moons, lost and lonely
above the concrete canyons. We made our daughter under shadows
broken blue as a flute's slant riff across the marvelous city.

Years later we found the Roman moon a weathered coin,
the Florentine, gold leaf—and Dublin's nightshining
part of the Liffey's argentine.

Pete's Canyon in Montana held a day-moon
ghosting a sunlit noon, a crescent of smoke—
just then a sudden hailstorm pocked the clearing with white stones.

> *—just here the words fail, fall, can't stay*
> *as you couldn't stay for this poem's still*
> *unfinished end.*
> *You died instead.*
> *And something has to take the place of white space*

so like the blank my life's impossibly become, all fifty-fo
of our years together gone—and who now can rememb
them with me? Your last hour was almost midnight,
your last breath shallow on the hand I held to you
as I breathed out "I've loved you my whole life,
even before I met you." A thing so true and strange
I wasn't sure I'd heard my own voice say it.

Coming home after your death, the moon stopped me,
was nearly as radiant as daylight—so oddly not
the cold light a full moon casts,
but a half moon bright as day, some new
kind of broken wafer overhead.

              Later, I would learn
the planets were in rare alignment on just that date,
like obedient marchers placing a new complexion
on the night that gave me also
a red fox wearing its own unearthly glow
where the moon gave back, like memory,
the sun that made it and the stranger
morning that would come.

Vulpine

May 10, 2011

> Yet here was the thing in the midst of the bones,
> the wide-eyed innocent fox inviting me to play . . .
> The universe was swinging around in some fantastic
> fashion to present its face . . .
>> —Loren Eiseley, *The Unexpected Universe*

My love, I would set you again on that trail you loved
to run, your hair still long from another era,
your heart the beat, your mind all music—
Getz, Parker, Bach, Gillespie,
Debussy, Stravinsky, Coltrane—your own
improvisations running alongside,
racing, shaping what your fingers
would play into the wind.

I remember April I remember you

                         I remember
how you lay curled in pain, your spine
collapsing like a column of smoke,
                    your hands
knotted with arthritis that took the flute
out of your grasp, but not the spirit of it, and not
the love you had for me, which depth
I've realized late, able to see it only in the daily dark
that is your absence—disappearance so immense
there's no measure, no image for it—
how the meaning of life is life, and the meaning
of death is life, no delusion intervening
in that tight-woven tapestry, no uplifting
wing.
              Only the fox came

on the night you died, strange
angel the color of gold fire,
                              trickster lifted
whole from a child's picture book,
lifting its delicate feet in the winespill
of moonlight that held the whole backyard
hostage to clarity. The planets
in rare, perfect alignment altered
this one night with light uncanny
as the fox that danced straight toward me.
Eyes full of that moon, he danced almost
close enough to touch, danced as if
to music, as if the animal would speak
in that language some single thing
not available elsewhere:
                              beauty, perhaps,
which may be holy and once only
and all we have.

The Widow's House

seems to be coming apart—pieces
of wall, snatches of a rug, chair-rungs,
shingles, plumbing, lamps, and doorknobs.
Glass shatters from rows of still-framed
faces. The mirrors are dusking over,
no longer disclosing.

                    Everything floats
as if gravity has left the place. It's not
violent; it is a loosening, a soundless
disengagement. Even her body has become
otherwise, flesh that can no longer
recognize itself.

Perhaps it is she who has gone to ash,
gone to ground and the dark.
She has asked so hard for him,
crying out in the night, weeping into
pots on the stove, roses in the yard.

Perhaps she is the ghost
in the house they built dissolving,
turning now as if in the grip of a slowed
tornado, air full of what could be
confetti in some kind of decelerating
celebration: music, books, conversations
shredding in the wind that memory
always becomes—unfastened, recasting,
disheveling as the end of lovemaking.
She sits on a splintering floor,
surrounded by the done-for.

The Widow Tries to Say It without Philosophy, Theology, or Grief

Even as we lived in certain rooms
(lamp on that table, the curtains' tassel-ties,
antique clock, framed Audubon)
things were shifting, taking place
in some sheer other dimension we

couldn't know, our lives taken as if by a horse-drawn
caravan rocking at breakneck speed through landscapes sped
to all-and-nothing:
                    falling trees become saplings newly
                      sprung through snow and butterflies; October's
                      brilliant leaves adrift over February's crocus—

and that caravan? Is it sorcerers, soothsayers, thieves
wearing our own quick-change faces? driving
what unseen horses, harrows, houses?
as the lamp on *this* table flickers, and this
chair and this cup dim—

it isn't death I'm bringing up but another
derangement: something out of the Brothers Grimm
dislimning the known, the held world,
with abandon we don't see the way
we can't see the hour-hand at its errand.

Why is it, then, we never took photographs of rooms
we lived in, their tackle and trim, their blurring
breath; never captured the roses on the vase
by the stairs, the bed with its jigsaw quilt,
noon's slab of sunlight on a hand-hooked rug—

though a corner of kitchen may show in a snapshot
of a birthday cake, or part of a sofa
with the baby on it, or a fireplace somebody's
leaning against—but no whole, no context full
of the matter we made our days among—

and even if we had captured such shadows, we would
nevertheless have lost how it felt to turn at the banister,
pass the hall mirror, to walk through the air
of that doorway—
                        the caravan speeding away

with what memory can't hold
which is still, after all, everything
that already was *not there* even as we sat
together at dinner with everyone caught
in the bright flash, our glasses raised to this.

The Widow Remembers That Someone Once Said

All The Important Questions Can be Asked in the Words of a Child

What is it all about?
As if this were a story or a play,
I asked the gods and the trees, the sun
transforming figures in stained glass.

Now I know it's only ever out-
of-order, the answer not at home—
and you, my love, gone out,
taken by eclipse. It turns about
how entirely now the meaning's in
your death, the one that has become
my mother's, my father's, my friends'.
Every going fused into the one
twilight shadow like a stalled raptor's.

Take away the beautiful things
and the words that wake them:
the river heron, Judas trees in Greece,
the April moon's face everywhere—
all that music, desire, your hands on me
whatever might have lived in us in grace.
                    Pour memory on the ground;
that is not
what it's about, not what
it's about
at all.

The Widow Reverses Wordsworth

Bliss it was in that dawn to be alive,
But to be young was very heaven!
    —William Wordsworth

January 2012

    Yes, bliss and very heaven, all
that I couldn't see for some desire or minor
fury at a slight, some shiny distraction.
Back then, a long forgetfulness like rain
dropped over me, a grievous gray
unnoticing—how warm, how close, loose,
lovely the living body, how dear, how much
the world.

But is this not heaven too, *now* to be alive?
Even in solitary, in the absence here
on the winter porch open to birds
cutting the morning to gold ribbons,
breaking day into music, this day
chill and light and mine?

Last night, the January moon
was a slender bowl, Venus near over it
as if to pour starlight into that silver cup—
so clear, so sharp under the hammer of cold.
I noticed that; why can't I love it?

Or the early blooming winter Daphne
sweetly open, its fragrance spun
across an afternoon, nothing if not
very heaven—this time not youth

but *knowing*—death and being
in light and air and wings, in the squirrel's
scribbling in the oak's bare fringe of twigs.

My gone love, this word-picturing is
only a kind of Braille for the abundance
I own but cannot read, veiled as it is
with what can't be retrieved.
Instead, I've gathered your death
around me like an iron shawl, the light
battered back, the birds only shrieks
in a season of no stars.
      Or might this poem
be only semaphore, guide
for the closer sure approach
of my own dying, bringing the sudden

knowledge that *this day,* this very day
seeming to say *without, without,*
is bliss the fog of memory obscures—
the very picture
     of world that ever
was and never can be here.

The Widow Finds the Annuals

Some call them yearbooks, these collections
of postage-stamp-sized portraits. No one would browse
such histories. *Out of the house!*
I say aloud, since nobody's here, detritus

of your long, just-ended life and mine still trudging on.
Such titles they boasted: *Pirates' Cove*
for the football team so much beloved
when your college was small and full of 1949.

Wolf's Den names my high school senior year,
a gathering of children beginning our last stand.
And here's 1953, your first teaching year out West—
Deming, New Mexico High—hairdos and the marching band.

On blank back pages or under the compressed faces
our scrawled notes: good luck wishes and confident affections
everybody wrote to everybody. There's no place
for perennials here, no return in such reflections,

these stalled mirrors blossoming at the cliff's edge,
where something was about to happen, something about
the everything we'd be. Until we're not.
As you are not, my love, nor all your knowledge

of music and our dance. It's the oldest boring story
the young despise until it is their history
that's gone to seed in no season. Though I agreed
with myself to hold onto nothing but what I need

in my new life alone, I lift the bound
and faded shadows of our selves
and put them all together on the shelves.
Someone else will have to plow them under ground.

Clearing

July 2013

The morning after the hurricane of '96
knocked down all our big trees, some
just missing the house, a new light
lived here awhile. Every window held
a green presentment against unbroken glass.
We were embraced by treetops, high summer
downed around us. A transformed noon sun
came indoors, verdant with history.

Now the sky over this house
is no longer open; only one ribbon
of uninterrupted blue holds
above the chairs on the added deck,
where I lean back and look into another
July's pewter twilight pierced with swifts
and bats retracing their sonar maps
on the last of the day.
                              Absence and return
dance in a cloud of midges drunk on full summer.
The trees are as heavy as they ever were,
and I can no longer remember the sound of that wind,
   nor the great vacant sky after,
         nor how it felt to wonder how the birds
               had kept from dying, or the horses
in the stunned fields. I can't
                              remember the exact
blue of the unlikely butterfly that startled us that day,
rising out of a torn cardboard box in the garage,
that strange day, that *afterward*
not unlike this one:

             you dead three years,
gone into the sky's uncertain blue,
into this air that empties
around me again and again.

Reach

If you should reach out of the dark you have become

—and what is it? what is that black, that first thing,
and last, background and before-ground of stars?

if you could reach out to me as nothing but farthest
darkness; if you could hold it out and ask me to,
I'd put my hand into that shadow-hand and go.

Garment of Light

Resolve all the leaps of light.
—THEODORE ROETHKE

If Their Voices

Sacred Harp Singers, Georgia, 1930s

If their voices were visible entities
flying from the Deep South's fading
churches, startled from the throats
of an earlier century by hope revived,
they would be birds.

Ordinary starlings. Or swifts perhaps,
a flock of embers cohering, dispersing,
action-painting against cloud or blue, dissolving
form to dissolving form. Turn on turn
they clot and flow, shift like wind-tossed
silk across the sky, smoke
of the pumping hearts that hold
the wingbeats' bellows to the burn.

They make and remake,
unraveling and reweaving the garment of light
to puzzle all earthly suitors. They work
the air to patterns of redemption in a moving
kaleidoscope of contradiction. They are
voices reaching for nothing but heaven.

Watch this story of formal match and change.
Listen. It's neither language nor music but flesh
become no thing, word become space
where the missing third wrings open
and, as if designing, folds and folds
rough fugue into this world again.

Rising Star 1984

We'd passed a dozen side roads, traveling that stretch
of highway across Texas west to east by way of Dallas,
signs for tough small towns like *Clyde,*
Throckmorton, Comanche. But that day, incongruous
as song erupting from a prickly pear,
a sign for *Rising Star.*

We'd left Abilene in the dark, early to make time
past dreaming ranches. Only windmills were awake,
creaking water-anthems among cattle still as fence posts
just paling into view.
                              November sky
had turned gray with a trademark chill West Texas
dawn, and a numb horizon opened abruptly
beyond the bullet-pocked town sign.
On the single street, a stoplight danced in a little wind.
Oil wells whined along railroad tracks, black pumpjacks
lifting and falling, huge up close, grotesque versions
of the toy drinking birds I'd bought as souvenirs
forty years before, on this road with my father.

Breakfast in Rising Star, you said, *what better place?*
The cafe's wide glass window held images
painted on with thin, holiday paint that washes off,
so the glow from the interior shone through figures
of a running back gripping a football, behind him
a cheerleader with red pom-poms, and a large but tepid
American flag; *Go Wildcats* lettered underneath in black.

We sat on hard chairs listening to the talk
of ranchers, roughnecks, the guy from the car repair,
their voices washing over us with weather,
livestock prices, carburetors, and what to expect

at Friday night's championship game when Tank
Johnson's boy would surely bring it home.
After eggs and chili grits, we walked into full morning.

What I remember now is the light before,
spilling from painted plate glass, pools
of yellow light that was somehow old
as 1950's summers, paper lanterns, the sudden
drench of Saturday afternoon when the movie's
double-feature first lets out. So long ago, so far
it might as well have come
from any distant star.

—for B.H. Fairchild

Burnt Offerings

summer's flare on my father's
folly, an ornamental pond with fish like fugitive
firelight, their tails trailing fine as wind-struck smoke—
green flame of the live oak
spreading in sunset's arson, my swing hanging by two
rough ropes in a glittering stillness—
compacted coals
of a pomegranate broken open on the ground
and smoldering with birds—
deep-red embers in the silk
feathers of the rooster's back, slick in the rainy dawn
that unmuffles his alarm—
even the chill white blaze
of a March dogwood trapped into early radiance,
the tips of its blossoms scorched with legend—
surely memory's medium
is glass, fire's child molten, poured
into form that can focus like a lens, can fix the sun's
dalliance, inexplicable and *inknown,*
on gone flesh or leaf, on lost house or hand,
on the vanished music or stopped breath
to ignite original dazzle, then
shattering, then ash.

Pastoral

Empty hayrick, nineteenth-century barn
fields unfurling toward late spring, light rain
in the unbroken dark, a little thunder
way off toward the west horizon.

New green tractor beside the decrepit one
he still uses because a wren has built in the new
machine and he refuses to disturb her.
Red pickup still ticking beside the house.

He's just come from last shift at the welding job
he has to keep if he would save this farm.
He's young, married not long, his wife
out this night with girlfriends, gone

until late. He steps into the brief gold
of the porch light, whistles up the dog, commences
in small rain the errand he's bent upon.
Perhaps a goat is stuck in the back pasture fence,

or something to do with the pond he dug with his father
who died last year, their great project stocked at last
with catfish, bream, a few bass. There's some thing
he means to tend. Or he's just walking the land, checking,

the way lovers do. Perhaps he hums, or speaks
to the dog dancing beside him or leaping ahead,
and the dark sky comes closer until the dog barks to call
attention and they turn back toward the house that was

his great-grandfather's, now his to rescue, and with it
the acres he has chosen to be his life.
Already he has rebuilt the fences, keeps chickens,
breeds goats, plants a garden and a sweet potato field.

What might he be thinking as the storm breaks
into sticks of flame above him? His wife
hears weather news and stops the car
on a roadside, waiting out hard rain.

In a few minutes she turns for home. Nothing
of what is the case is in her mind or can be so.
Maybe she thinks she'll tell him how it looked
almost like one fire, the streaks of lightening

close as clashing swords, and the sound a roar.
She's almost there. The house lights, fogged
by diminishing rain, are all on.
What she can't imagine is why the doors

are open, the dog drenched and running in and out,
her husband not answering her calls into a now
perfectly still black night in which he is facedown
in pasture mud, pinned by the sky's deadbolt,

the cloud's bright nail—she will call
until almost dawn with the rest of the searchers,
the storm over, and the wren still settled
warm on the nest.

—for Steven

After Despair

let things be spare
and words for things be thin
as the slice of moon
the loon's cry snips;
as the cape of dusk
that clothes the swift;
as the brief shim
that rims eclipse.

Colloquy

Superstition, like belief, must die,
And what remains when disbelief has gone?
    —from "Church Going" by Philip Larkin

I asked the creatures of grass and air,
the web-weavers and jumpers; inquired
of broken sticks and pebbles worn smooth
in the long hyperbole of water.
I asked the trees and their wreaths of birds;
queried mouse, cougar, possum, deer.
I questioned even the deep halls where a congress
of weather and roots holds April a political prisoner.

But there was no word in earth's house.
Bare branches held a crooked sky
without story or prophecy, and the stone
was a deaf mirror.

To love the world that cannot answer
is to give your children to silence,
to the beautiful instructions of millennia
uttered only once, then ringing
far and clear and perfectly
inaudible as the stars.

To love the world that cannot answer
takes losing. It takes us
all our lives.

Song for Mary Ellen

She loved to watch them, hummingbirds
drawn to the sweet red of the feeder
and to the real fire of her husband's flowers.
Gilded with summer, they hovered, gemstones
turning on the silk streamers
of the morning rising.

She brought the brilliant cardinals to her,
and the chickadees, the loud jays and shy
wrens, the purple-breasted finches.
And always she fed the pet rooster—named *Floppy*
because his crowning comb drooped low.

She forgot no one. Perhaps the birds were heartbeat,
ardent messengers of the spirit, here to stun
us into seeing how bright-winged is time,
how full the world that has in it such startling
flights, such saving flowering, even such
flagging crowns as ours. She fed us too.
And then she flew.

Ode to a Shawl

Butterflies would kiss
this weave in which the garden breathes,
colors binding with shadow in a dance, a sheave

of delicacy blooming bloodred, tenacity
in a sudden silver web strung from the fingers
of an artist whose name I'll never know,

a woman who has put into this garment the laughter
of children and the wounds that will find them,
sunrise and starlit gamut of desire and loss.

And what to say of the plain brown running through—
its color of dirt, color of the thrush who sings
the whole earth's palette, even

the ways of war and time. Cain and angels interlaced
in silk, in wool and linen, some in frail ribbons,
some sturdy as homespun, all trailing long and long

such fringes as might inhabit a separate plane.
They sway the way light tethered
to a candle-flame can sway a room.

What of the woman who imagined it, who made it,
and the women who held it, wore it,
then folded and handed it on, an elegance,

a bazaar: strange, home-warm surround
of light still humming with the dark.

—for Barbara

Office Cubicle

She is trying to imagine Spain in this windowless place
whose florescent light is disabused of all shadow.
Surely the rich sun-spill in that country
would be better than money; would hold
close the dark outlines of music and old blood.
There, houses whiter than the baptized would cast
their night-likenesses on the stones of afternoons
full of rough wine and goat-cries.

Someone has told her the potted plant beside her
can live in a room without even a blind-slit of sun
for years. *Light years,* she thinks. She's trying
to give it better directions—the map of Spain
for instance—instead of the spaceship's
path to Mars, so that this growing thing may flower
at least once for the sake of the earth's journey
and the memory of stars.

The Drifter Picked Up at the Dump

Here was the place police could never push you farther than.
A fire, a little wine, deep sleep.

Picked up drunk at dawn among piles of trash,
you were lifted out of dream, and fed
into a slot. What happened was a squashed-
solid package smaller than a jail cell.

Machines that process junk know nothing of appeals,
but an operator glimpsed the loophole where your head,
all wild mouth, yelled until
you were sprung from locked scrap, miracle
with nothing worse than a broken shoulder
and a couple of lines in the newspapers.

The things we've got to beware of
get bolder and bolder.

Ode to a Guinea Pig

Borrowing from Kierkegaard,
I love this animal because he is absurd.
A small mammal lacking all ambition,
he carries no heavy affectations of joy.
His whistle is sharp and singular, and only
for food. It makes an honest music.

He does not lie to us.
I am here is the one communication
in his Buddha-sitting, his fat-assed waddle.
The only surprise he offers is the occasional dash,
faster than you'd imagine,
to nowhere in particular.
He's no wild thing, yet not quite tame.

His name is of no interest to him. *Don't*
call me, he could be saying. I'd guess his DNA
has nothing of the pig, the rabbit, fox, or cow.
Perhaps he's related to the long thoughts
of philosophers; or is a creature of his own
imagining—a plump baby god watching over
an attenuated world.

He loves us as he is able, comprehending
warmth and softness, lettuce leaves and hay.
He understands snug openings. He embodies
the poet's admonition not to *mean*
but to *be* (and also Hamlet's but without
the *or not* part).

There's no creature like him because he has dreamed
no such thing. We should take note of him,
bask in that steady gaze, and learn.

—for Mollie

Parking Lot

This pocked gray pavement, a sky
about to storm—the lights come on
early, as if for a game
in a summer stadium. A small crowd
is holding its breath. Suddenly with me,
simple and tricky as water, here
is the smell of a book I read once
in a room whose windows were open.
Someone speaks there in a voice like iron.
Someone is asking me not to go on.

I go on reading, chewing a strand of my hair
in the habit of childhood. There's rain
in the window, tasseled furniture in the room,
and some vast errand I can't put off.

On the pavement a dead cardinal
is a bright dropped fan staining
asphalt reflected in a gray sky,
a bell falling to silence.
I can taste the bitter ends of the story
I own but do not understand.

Photography 3
on photographs by Bill Wittliff

You call it *tragaluz,* which means *drinking light*—
photographing with pin-hole cameras, the first
image catchers.
        Homemade is best, perhaps
because it retains the early touch and makes
the means of the gamble material, as in building
an animal trap.

Depending on subject and intent,
the camera size will vary.
Some artists make more than a hundred
different punctured boxes
for capturing what no machine can see.

What is swallowed is taken in
through one tiny opening, is spread in time, with time,
as time—dragging light through the primitive
gateway so slowly as to measure the other worlds
carried by every being, every object, every landscape—
burgeon and veil—around, behind, within. Here's
afterimage, before-sight, aura, robe of the hitherto
otherwise.

This way of capturing is more like memory
or more like dream, since memory becomes dream
dragged through the shrinking portal of a life,
a flaring, obscuring, haunting. One picture
in particular: the wolf's head created
by movement of wind in leaves of an oak tree,
portrait of motion in a twilight's draining
borderland—spirit animal, ghost,
the more-than-there.

Survivals

Burying Ground, East Texas, 2005

The red clay road that brings us has deepened
with almost two hundred years of ox and cart, horses, wagons,
log trucks, pickups, drilling-rig haulers. It has been
gouged down in some places so far that the earth rises
on either side of our car five feet or more,
dried-blood colored walls that hug what passes—it's one way—
as if there might be no route out of here.

We've come like tourists seven miles into backwoods
to see the place, passing just one house the color
of the remnant mule standing inside a stove-in fence.
A well in the front yard, the tin roof almost new, two
white plastic chairs on the tilted porch—it could be
a mirage, or a grainy, colorless photograph pinned
against the giant oak behind it.

We're coming to the heart of something
in Shelby County, Texas, something brought
across millennia and continents to make in this forest
a moonscape, which to see is as startling as finding
desert in a river rapids or a stone wall in the sky.

The graveyard was here first.
A little church, dingy but sturdy, came much later.
First here's the small hill's pinkish-gray soil
bare of any weed or grass blade, and holding
perhaps a hundred dead dating from the 1830s
to the present, in rough family groups.
Their bare ground brings to mind *scorched earth*
which the careful patterns, raked and swept, deny.

Called raked graveyards or swept cemeteries, they're
mostly white Protestant. Very few are left.
Silence here is real. No engine hum however distant,
only birds and the scribbling of small forest animals
among pine and hardwoods carefully fenced away.
We're standing still as statuary in late afternoon's tarnished light.

In this space all roads converge.
The three of us fan out along the winding paths.
Every grave is neatly mounded west to east,
earth piled high and sometimes spined
with seashells or broken bricks. They stand
like proud flesh, like scars.

Pathways between are designed to carry
rain away, and after rain must be raked anew
into swirled rhythms that could be excerpts
from some Asian garden. The mounds too
must be rightly shaped again.
There are no crosses.

Some headstones bear a carved rose
or a lamb; most are plain names and dates
on ordinary fieldstone. A few have epitaphs:
She Finished Her Row or *Taken to be a Angel*
or *As I Am So Ye Shall Be.* Some are ancient
wood, names erased by weather, their charges
tended with the rest.

No vines. No weeds. No grass. No bush or flower
except along the inside fence-line whose corners
are held by cedars. Here are Demeter's

roses that belong also to the Magna Mater,
straight-lined against the fence where Ishtar's
irises and Hera's lilies also sing Mary
Queen of Heaven to a relic spring.

By the lich-gate, junipers and hollies reach evergreen
toward ever after. Inside, and only against the strict fence,
the oldest goddess plays in all her banished guises.

Broken pottery dishes are half-buried
in the mounded earth, joining barren to the flowering
in practices from African, European, and Native
American rituals combined, taking in even the broken
glass bottles propped in front of markers
to declare departure of spirits.
                                        Grave gifts recall them:
a rusting jackknife, a keepsake necklace, shotgun shells,
an umbrella, a doll, a toy drum, a mirror.

This earthen house of the hidden faces east
toward sunrise, and dusk steals over silence
cloaking grace and numinous reprise.

Articles of Faith

There is another world and it is in this one.
—Paul Eluard

A spider set her wheel in the frame of our kitchen window,
fragile and singular as a snowflake, an imperfect circular
knowledge of light, of dew and shadow. Its capture
of purest brevity endures the span of one whole October

fifty years ago.

The dead pin oak stood sentry on a rise
of my childhood's farm, and wouldn't fall.
I dreamed its roots leafed underground, keeping
seasons where heaven surely was. Against all reason

it stood decades, black against the sun.
I knew the swift's invisible tower rising, its making
all sheer will and lift, turn after torn turn, higher, higher
until I could almost see the architecture of that motion,
veil of circles connecting as smoke connects,

the soul of the fire that makes it.
Dusty straw nests, a smell like ashes. The unkempt hen-yard
was robed in a rare, light snow, runic scratches in the dirt
filling, lilting into white. What would I have done without
such transformations? Not angels but a turning round

to light's garden, a warm egg in my hand.

Has dark a garden? What's given is complete, if only
in our unseeing. What of the jackfish? Inch-long larval
worms with mandibles, they lived in straight-down holes
and would grasp any lowered weed-stem so violently
we children pulled them into killing sun and marveled.

The panther's haunting song stayed in my father's ear,
a sound to match his life's mourning.
Hunter of anything wild: deer, fox, pheasant, he hoped
also for the panther in a tree, the one we dare not know—

the animal that cries out like a child—

the one that matches. And does not match.
A poet once said we must fall in love outward.
Fall in love then, and know the cost of
loving starfish and quartz,
hummingbirds and meteors—their kinship, their
distance. Fall for the frogs, the bats, the elephants,
the great cats, all the sacrificed dying out.

Learn those fervent silences.

For Eucharist, take into your mouth
a bee, a pebble, a thorn, a weathered
bone, a worm, a hen-feather, a violet. Take
onto your tongue the solitary panther's
scream and the streaming starlight. Drink
clay-reddened creek water and the black rain
in a rotting stump. Say
                         this is that
other world, afterlife
                         and the before.

Take it and sing.

NOTES

"Poetry is a species of thought with which nothing else can be done."
The quotation on the title page of the first section of this book is from
Howard Nemerov's essay "Thirteen Ways of Looking at a Skylark."

"Resolve all the leaps of light."
The quotation on the title page of the third section of this book is from
Straw for the Fire: From the Notebooks of Theodore Roethke, edited by
David Wagoner.

"If Their Voices"
The *Sacred Harp* is music sung, unaccompanied by, the entire congrega-
tion in poor rural churches of the Deep South. Its American roots are in
New England, where it died out early on. Its deeper roots are in Medieval
Europe, in the organum, the earliest form of harmony. The human voice
is considered the Sacred Harp, and the singers do not use even a tuning
fork, tuning only to each other. The *Songbook,* published in Dothan, Ala-
bama, in 1902 shows the notes in geometric shapes, a completely different
system of notation. The harmony is harsh, with a missing third, and the
structure is very often fuge-like. With a forceful beat and an unsubtle and
often unvaried volume, the music is powerful and rough; it possesses a
haunting quality both joyful and dark. The poem describes the sound of
untrained voices recorded in churches of the 1930s, at a time when my
maternal grandfather was "singing master" of his small church in Mt.
Enterprise, Texas.

"Photography 3"
The poem is a response to the book *La Vida Brinca* by Bill Wittliff. Best
known as a screenwriter, Wittliff is also widely known as a photographer,
often specializing in pinhole photography shot with very simple cameras
consisting of a closed oblong box (length depending on the user's intent)

having a pin-sized hole in one end and photographic paper or film at the other. Wittliff makes his own cameras and has crafted more than a hundred. His work is haunting of time, a timelessness, or spread time. It requires exposures of several minutes or longer. His powerful work is centered mostly in West Texas and Mexico. The last stanza of the poem describes a photograph titled *Spirit Animal.* The term *tragaluz* is Spanish for "drinking light."

"Joe Mike"
Two italicized lines are from "Prayer" by George Herbert and from Theodore Roethke's "The Shimmer of Evil"—itself a quotation from Louise Bogan's poem of that title.

"Survivals"
Considered southern folk cemeteries, the swept (or scraped or raked) graveyards are nineteenth-century survivals. The cemetery in the poem is in deep East Texas near Louisiana, an area settled early by homesteaders from southern states. Studies show that these cemeteries, mostly white and Protestant, demonstrate influences from West Africa, Medieval England, Mediterranean Europe, and Native America.

"The Drifter Picked Up at the Dump"
The poem is an elaboration of a brief story in a 1970's newspaper I found in an old file, minus the exact date and the name of the newspaper.

CPSIA information can be obtained
at www.ICGtesting.com
Printed in the USA
LVOW12s0016150917

548750LV00003B/364/P